CANTON DEPOT

MARTIN BRAY

AMBERLEY

About the Author

My interest in railways started at the age of six when my father used to drop me off on his way to work at the level crossing near Bognor Regis railway station. My passion for railways led me into an engineering apprenticeship with one of the most respected manufacturers of railway locomotives, Ruston Diesels Limited, in 1973. I had spotted all of the British Railways locomotives in the old Ian Allan pocketbook by 1976 and photographed them all by 1985. I qualified as a chartered engineer in 1987 and was head-hunted to South Wales in 1989, which was the start of a very close relationship with staff at Canton and Margam depots and still continues today, although both facilities have long closed. My retirement in December 2019 has enabled me to spend more time photographing the decline of locomotives in France and on landscape photography in the Canary Islands.

First published 2024

Amberley Publishing
The Hill, Stroud
Gloucestershire, GL5 4EP

www.amberley-books.com

ISBN 978 1 3981 0384 9 (print)
ISBN 978 1 3981 0385 6 (ebook)

British Library Cataloguing in Publication Data.
A catalogue record for this book is available from the British Library.

Origination by Amberley Publishing.
Printed in the UK.

Introduction

Canton Traction Maintenance Depot (Canton TMD) was rebuilt and officially opened on 18 September 1964, and its fleet initially consisted of Class 08 shunting locomotives, Class 14 and Class 35 Diesel Hydraulic Locomotives, and Class 37 and Class 47 diesel electric locomotives.

It provided motive power in the Cardiff and Valleys areas for passenger and freight traffic. Class 08 locomotives could be found in most depots, yards and sidings, shunting all types of rolling stock. Class 14 diesel hydraulic locomotives were used for local freight trip working.

During its lifetime Canton TMD also maintained a fleet of Class 03, 20, 25, 46 and 56 locomotives, all of which have now left, ultimately leaving a fleet of Class 08/09, 60, 66 and 67 locomotives.

The facilities at Canton TMD included heavy maintenance, capable of undertaking power unit changes and a running shed that was used for carrying out servicing and routine maintenance work. It was also supported by a Ground Wheel Lathe for re-profiling of locomotive, carriage and wagon wheelsets and a Load Bank for testing locomotive power units. The depot also operated a 75-ton Cowans Sheldon crane which was used locally and nationally for re-railing purposes.

From time to time the depot also undertook refurbishment and modification work to Class 08, 37, 56, 60 and 67 locomotives and Royal Mail coaching stock.

Canton TMD became part of Transrail in 1994, following the broadly regional split of British Rail's Trainload Freight Operations and in 1996 Transrail was acquired by English, Welsh & Scottish Railway.

There was a very close working relationship between Canton TMD and its customers which resulted in a hire contract during 1996 to supply Allied Steel and Wire Limited with five Class 08 shunting locomotives, three of which were equipped with remote control. The locomotives were driven by Allied Steel & Wire drivers but maintained by Canton TMD. The contract was extremely challenging due to the environment that they were being used in, especially those locomotives that were fitted with remote control, and monthly meetings were held between Canton TMD and Allied Steel & Wire to monitor the contract. These very challenging conditions brought about a very fast turnover of locomotives, which was a rich source of interest to railway enthusiasts.

A similar relationship was developed with Valley Lines, which initially resulted in a hire contract to supply Class 37/4 locomotives during Rugy Internationals and ultimately to supply two rush-hour services between Cardiff and Rhymney with Class 37/4 locomotives around 1998.

During 2001 Canton TMD formed a Shunter Gang consisting of a Team Leader and six Level 5 fitters with a specific objective of maintaining the Great Western fleet of Class 08/09 shunting locomotives in prime working order, thereby minimising the need to transport them back to the depot by road for repairs. The Shunter Gang were also responsible for the unofficial hand-painted names of former workmates that were embellished below the cab windows.

During April 2002, two months prior to Allied Steel & Wire going into receivership, Canton TMD stored five Class 37 locomotives, 37403/406/417/425/898, in Tremorfa Works. Two of these locomotives, 37406/417, later became part of an F exam project with 37422 at Canton Depot.

The success of the Valley Lines contract resulted in three Class 37/4 locomotives, 37406/417/422, receiving an F exam at Canton TMD during 2002 and 2003. 37422 was the first to emerge during January 2003 and was officially named *Cardiff Canton* at a ceremony held at Canton TMD on 31 January 2003. Some concern was shown by staff that the F exam should have included the removal of the crankshaft to enable new main bearings to be fitted. However, during January 2004, 37422 Canton Depot suffered a major mechanical failure with a collapsed main bearing and with the impending closure of Canton TMD, it was sent to Toton TMD for a power unit change. The power unit from 37422 was removed and its alternator was attached to the engine from long-stored 37220 which had relatively low engine hours. A spate of technical issues and failure on a Pathfinders Rail tour on 2 May 2005 led to its power unit being replaced at Toton TMD with that from accident-damaged and withdrawn 37408.

Class 08 08951 was refurbished and named *Fred*, at a ceremony held on 21 July 2003. The locomotive was named after and attended by Fred Billet, a retired fitter.

English, Welsh & Scottish Railway sponsored the Railway Horse weekend at the Severn Valley Railway on 7 June 2003, and Canton TMD repainted 60089 for the event, where it was named *The Railway Horse*. 37422 *Cardiff Canton* also attended the event and headed up the evening supper train where it was sadly announced that the company had lost the Royal Mail contract.

On Sunday 30 May 2004, Canton TMD finally closed its doors nearly forty years after its reopening on 18 September 1964. The closure was brought about by the reduction in rail traffic due to the loss of the Royal Mail contract, closure of Ebbw Vale and Allied Steel & Wire steelworks, contraction at Llanwern steelworks and general excess of maintenance capacity in the company.

A majority of Canton TMD staff were transferred to Margam Depot, some moved to other locations, including train-operating companies, and some took voluntary redundancy.

37422, formerly D6966 and 37266.

08350, formerly D3420, was built in Crewe Works during 1957. It is pictured in British Rail blue livery on 19 June 1983 and was scrapped by Rod Hull during 2010.

08351, formerly D3421, was built in Crewe Works during 1957. It is pictured in blue livery on 13 March 1981 and was scrapped in Swindon Works during 1986.

08352, formerly D3422, was built in Crewe Works during 1957. It is pictured in British Rail blue livery on 19 June 1983 and was scrapped in Swindon Works during 1986.

08375, formerly D3460, was built in Darlington Works during 1957. It is pictured in blue livery on 22 March 1992 and is now owned by Port of Boston Limited.

08466, formerly D3581, was built in Crewe Works during 1958. It is pictured in EWS livery on a low loader in the brickyard opposite Canton Depot on 23 December 1999 and was scrapped by C. F. Booth during 2011.

08466, formerly D3581, was built in Darlington Works during 1957 and is pictured in EWS livery and equipped with remote control on 12 August 2002. 08466 was named *Brillo* at Canton Depot after Mike Edgeworth, retired painter who used brillo pads for his paint preparation work. It was scrapped by C. F. Booth during 2011.

08479, formerly D3594, was built in Horwich Works during 1958. It is pictured in blue livery under maintenance on 19 April 1987 and is now privately owned at the East Lancashire Railway.

08479, formerly D3594, was built in Horwich Works during 1958. It is pictured in blue livery on 28 March 1993 and is now privately owned at the East Lancashire Railway.

08480, formerly D3595, was built in Horwich Works during 1958 and is pictured in non-standard green livery on 4 August 2002. 08480 was named *Ray* at Canton Depot after Ray Giles, a retired crane driver, and is now owned by Rail Support Services.

08480, formerly D3595, was built in Horwich Works during 1958. It is pictured in non-standard green livery on 14 July 2002 and is now owned by Rail Support Services.

08488, formerly D3603, was built in Horwich Works during 1958. It is pictured in blue livery on 19 April 1987 and was scrapped by M. C. Metals in 1991.

08499, formerly D3654, was built at Doncaster during 1958. It is pictured in undercoat on 4 June 2005 and is now owned by Pullman Rail.

08499, formerly D3654, was built in Horwich Works during 1958. It is pictured in EWS livery without numbers on 4 August 2004 and is now owned by Pullman Rail.

08576, formerly D3743, was built in Crewe Works during 1958. It is pictured in blue livery on 27 August 2001 and was scrapped by T. J. Thomson during 2007.

08589, formerly D3756, was built at Crewe Works during 1959. It is pictured in blue livery on 28 March 1983 and was scrapped by Gwent Demolition during 1994.

08651, formerly D3818, was built in Horwich Works during 1959 and is pictured in Departmental grey livery on 4 June 2005. 08651 was named *Fitzy* at Canton Depot after John Fitzgerald, retired fitter, and was scrapped by European Metal Recycling during 2011.

08653, formerly D3820, was built at Horwich Works during 1959 and is pictured in Railfreight Distribution livery on 10 September 2002. 08653 was fitted with ex-Southern Region high brake pipes and is now owned by Harry Needle Railroad Company.

08653, formerly D3820, was built at Horwich Works during 1959 and is pictured in Railfreight Distribution livery at Allied Steel & Wire Limited, Tremorfa Works, on 19 April 2002. 08653 was fitted with ex-Southern Region high-level brake pipes and is now owned by Harry Needle Railroad Company.

08660, formerly D3827, was built at Horwich Works during 1959. It is pictured in blue livery at the Open Day on 6 July 1985 and was scrapped by Gwent Demolition during 1994.

08664, formerly D3831, was built at Horwich Works during 1959. It is pictured in blue livery on 22 March 1992 and was scrapped by European Metal Recycling during 2012.

08734, formerly D3902, was built at Crewe Works during 1960. It is pictured in blue livery on 11 June 2000 and is now privately owned at the Dean Forest Railway.

08752, formerly D3920, was built at Crewe Works during 1960 and is pictured in ex-works EWS livery and equipped with remote control at Allied Steel & Wire, Tremorfa Works, on 7 August 2002. 08752 was named *Lenny* at Canton Depot after Len Tage, retired maintenance controller, and it is now owned by Rail Support Services Ltd.

08752, formerly D3920, was built at Crewe Works during 1960 and is pictured in Civil Engineers livery and equipped with remote control on 24 July 2001. 08752 was named *Brian* at Canton Depot after Brian Hammacott, retired fitter, and is now owned by Rail Support Services.

08786, formerly D3954, was built at Derby Works during 1960. It is pictured in Departmental grey livery on 28 March 1993 and is now owned by Harry Needle Railroad Company.

08792, formerly D3960, was built at Derby Works during 1960. It is pictured in Trainload Freight grey livery with Transrail markings on 14 October 1999 and was scrapped by T. J. Thomson during 2007.

08795, formerly D3963, was built at Derby Works during 1960 and is pictured in a non-standard Departmental grey livery on 22 March 1992. 08795 is now privately owned by the Llanelli & Mynydd Mawr Railway and on loan to Chrysalis Rail at Landore.

08801, formerly D3969, was built at Derby Works during 1960 and is pictured in blue livery with non-standard numbers on 2 September 2000. 08801 was named *T. L. Hannay* at Canton Depot after a retired shift supervisor and was scrapped at C. F. Booth during 2004.

08818, formerly D3986, was built at Derby Works during 1960. It is pictured in blue livery on 22 March 1992 and is now owned by Harry Needle Railroad Company.

08818, formerly D3986, was built at Derby Works during 1960. It is pictured in blue livery undergoing maintenance on 28 March 1993 and is now owned by Harry Needle Railroad Company.

08819, formerly D3987, was built at Derby Works during 1960. It is pictured in Departmental grey livery on 11 June 2000 and was scrapped by C. F. Booth during 2008.

08854, formerly D4022, was built at Horwich Works during 1960. It is pictured in EWS livery and equipped with remote control on 12 August 2002. 08854 was named *Bradshaw* at Canton Depot after Alan Bradshaw, retired fitter, and was scrapped by European Metal Recycling during 2012.

08856, formerly D4024, was built at Horwich Works during 1960 and is pictured in blue livery on 14 July 2002. 08856 was named *Lenny* at Canton Depot after Len Tage, retired maintenance controller, and was scrapped by T. J. Thompson during 2011.

08907, formerly D4137, was built at Horwich Works during 1962. It is pictured in non-standard black livery with cast number plates on 18 June 2001 and is now privately owned at the Great Central Railway.

08942, formerly D4172, was built at Darlington Works during 1962. It is pictured in blue livery on 28 March 1993 and was scrapped by T. J. Thomson during 2007.

08951, formerly D4181, was built at Darlington Works during 1962 and is pictured in ex-works EWS livery on 21 July 2003. 08951 was named *Fred* at Canton Depot after Fred Billet, retired fitter, and was scrapped by C. F. booth during 2011.

08954, formerly D4184, was built at Darlington Works during 1962. It is pictured in Trainload Freight livery with Transrail markings on 14 April 1996 and is now owned by Harry Needle Railroad Company.

08955, formerly D4185, was built at Darlington Works during 1962. It is pictured in Trainload Freight livery with Transrail markings on 11 June 2000 and was scrapped by C. F. Booth during 2009.

08957, formerly D4191, was built at Darlington Works during 1962. It is pictured in EWS livery on 30 December 2003 and was scrapped by Harry Needle Railroad Company during 2004. 08957 met its demise with a twisted frame in ex-works condition whilst on loan to Onllwyn Washery.

08994, formerly D3577 and 08462, built at Crewe Works during 1958 and rebuilt during 1985 with a lowered cab for use on the Burry Port & Gwendraeth Valley line. It is pictured in Departmental grey livery on 8 October 1994. 08994 was named *Gwendraeth* and is now privately owned by the Gwendraeth Railway Society.

09003, formerly D3667, was built at Darlington Works during 1959. It is pictured in EWS livery and equipped with buck-eye couplers on 3 December 2001. 09003 was named *Tattoo* at Canton Depot after Paul Keedwell, retired fitter's assistant, and was scrapped by European Metal Recycling during 2011.

09008, formerly D3719, was built at Darlington Works during 1959. It is pictured in part-painted EWS livery at Canton Brickyard opposite Canton Depot on 4 December 1998 and was scrapped by European Metal Recycling during 2011.

09008, formerly D3719, was built at Darlington Works during 1959 and is pictured in EWS livery on 17 June 2002. 09008 was named *Smudger* at Canton Depot after John Smith, retired plant fitter, and was scrapped by European Metal Recycling during 2011.

09016, formerly D4104, was built at Horwich Works during 1961 and is pictured in ex-works EWS livery on 7 October 2002. 09016 was named *The Sniper* at Canton Depot after Vince Dench, retired service shed technician, and was scrapped by European Metal Recycling during 2011.

09203, formerly D3949 and 08781, was built at Derby Works during 1960 and is pictured in Departmental grey livery on 12 May 2002. 09203 was named *Wrighty* at Canton Depot after George Wright, retired boilersmith, and was scrapped by C. F. Booth during 2012.

20087 and 20165, formerly D8087 and D8165, were respectively built by Robert Stephenson & Hawthorns Ltd during 1961 and English Electric Vulcan Foundry during 1966. 20087 is pictured in blue livery with red sole bar whilst 20165 is pictured in Railfreight grey livery on 2 April 1995. They spent a very short time at Canton Depot for trials at Aberthaw Power Station. 20087 is now owned by Harry Needle Railroad Company and 20165 was scrapped by Michael Douglas Ltd in 2001.

97201, formerly D5061, 24061 and TDB968007, was built at Crewe Works during 1960 and is pictured in Research Department red and blue livery at the Open Day on 6 July 1985. 97201 is now privately preserved at the North Yorkshire Moors Railway.

25035, formerly D5185, was built at Darlington Works during 1963. It is pictured in blue livery on 14 March 1981 and is now privately preserved at the Great Central Railway.

26038, formerly D5338, was built by Birmingham Railway & Carriage Company during 1959. It is pictured in undercoat on 30 October 2005 and is currently undergoing preservation at the Bo'ness & Kinneil Railway.

31452, formerly D5809, 31279 and 31552, was built by Brush Traction during 1961 and is pictured in Fragonset livery on 30 August 2000. 31452 was named *Minotaur* and is now owned by Eastern Rail Services.

31602, formerly D5614 and 31191, was built by Brush Traction during 1960 and is pictured in Fragonset livery on 13 October 1999. 31602 was named *Chimera* and was scrapped by RMS Locotec during 2018.

33008, formerly D6508, was built by Birmingham Railway Carriage and Wagon Company during 1960 and is pictured in blue livery at the Open Day on 6 July 1985. 33008 was named *Eastleigh* and is now privately preserved at the Battlefield Line.

33025, formerly D6543, was built by Birmingham Railway Carriage & Wagon Railway during 1960 and is pictured in Civil Engineers livery on 22 May 1998 with 33008. 33025 was named *Sultan* and is now owned by the West Coast Railways.

37023, formerly D6723, was built by English Electric Vulcan Foundry during 1961 and is pictured in Mainline livery on 4 September 1999. 37023 was named Stratford TMD Quality Approved and is now privately owned at the Pontypool & Blaenavon Railway.

37031, formerly D6731, was built by English Electric Vulcan Foundry during 1961. It is pictured in Railfreight Distribution livery on 14 April 1996 and was scrapped by M. R. J. Phillips during 1997.

37043, formerly D6743, was built by English Electric Vulcan Foundry during 1962. It is pictured in Civil Engineers livery with Transrail markings on 7 October 1998 and was scrapped by Sims Metals during 2003.

37051, formerly D6751, was built by English Electric Vulcan Foundry during 1962 and is pictured in EWS livery on 4 September 1999 with 37023. 37051 was named *Merehead* and was scrapped by Sims Metals during 2008.

37053, formerly D6753, was built by English Electric Vulcan Foundry during 1962. It is pictured in Railfreight Distribution livery on 11 July 1993 and was scrapped by C. F. Booth during 2006.

37058, formerly D6758, was built by English Electric Vulcan Foundry during 1962. It is pictured in Civil Engineers livery on 9 July 1998 and was scrapped by C. F. Booth during 2009.

37080, formerly D6780, was built by Robert Stephenson & Hawthorns during 1962. It is pictured in Trainload Freight Petroleum sector livery on 14 April 1996 and was scrapped by M. R. J. Phillips during 1997.

37107, formerly D6807, was built by English Electric Vulcan Foundry during 1963. It is pictured in Railfreight Distribution livery on 11 July 1993 and was scrapped by EWS during 1998.

37127, formerly D6827, was built by Robert Stephenson & Hawthorns during 1963. It is pictured in blue livery undergoing maintenance on 19 April 1987 and was scrapped by C. F. Booth during 2005.

37138, formerly D6838, was built by English Electric Vulcan Foundry during 1963. It is pictured in Trainload Freight Metals sector livery on 28 March 1993 and was scrapped by Harry Needle Railroad Company during 2004.

37180, formerly D6880, was built by Robert Stephenson & Hawthorns during 1963. It is pictured in blue livery undergoing maintenance on 19 June 1983 and was scrapped by European Metal Recycling during 2011.

37187, formerly D6887, was built by Robert Stephenson & Hawthorns during 1963. It is pictured under maintenance at the Open Day on 6 July 1985 and was scrapped by C. F. Booth in 2013.

37212, formerly D6912, was built by English Electric Vulcan Foundry during 1963. It is pictured in Trainload Freight Coal sector livery on 22 March 1992 and was scrapped by EWS during 2004.

37217, formerly D6917, was built by English Electric Vulcan Foundry during 1963. It is pictured in blue livery on 22 April 1989 and is now owned by Network Rail and has been renumbered 97304.

37222 formerly D6922, was built by English Electric Vulcan Foundry during 1963. It is pictured in Trainload Freight livery with Mainline sector markings on a low loader in the brickyard sidings opposite Canton Depot on 16 October 2002. 37222 was scrapped by T. J. Thomson during 2008.

37222 formerly D6922, was built by English Electric Vulcan Foundry during 1963. It is pictured in Trainload Freight livery with Mainline sector markings on 11 June 2000 and was scrapped by T. J. Thomson during 2008.

37223, formerly D6923, was built by English Electric Vulcan Foundry during 1963. It is pictured in Trainload Freight Coal sector livery on 19 June 1993 and was scrapped by Sims Metal during 2003.

37225, formerly D6925, was built by English Electric Vulcan Foundry during 1963. It is pictured in Trainload Freight livery without sector markings on 11 June 2000 and was scrapped by C. F. Booth during 2004.

37229, formerly D6929, was built by English Electric Vulcan Foundry during 1963. It is pictured in Trainload Freight Coal sector livery on 6 May 1995 and was scrapped by C. F. Booth during 2013.

37248, formerly D6948, was built by English Electric Vulcan Foundry during 1964 and is pictured in Trainload Freight Metals sector livery on 1 May 1994. 37248 is now preserved by the Growler Group at the Gloucester Warwickshire Railway.

37248, formerly D6948, was built by English Electric Vulcan Foundry during 1964 and is pictured in Trainload Freight Metals sector livery on 29 December 1991. 37248 is now preserved by the Growler Group at the Gloucester Warwickshire Railway.

37254, formerly D6954, was built by English Electric Vulcan Foundry during 1964. It is pictured in blue livery at the Open Day on 6 July 1985 and is now owned by Colas Rail.

37264, formerly D6964, was built by English Electric Vulcan Foundry during 1964. It is pictured in Civil Engineers livery on 7 July 1999 and is privately preserved on the North Yorkshire Moors Railway.

37278, formerly D6978, was built by English Electric Vulcan Foundry during 1965. It is pictured in blue livery on 23 July 1978 and was scrapped by T. J. Thomson during 2003.

37280, formerly D6980, was built by English Electric Vulcan Foundry during 1965. It is pictured in Trainload Freight Petroleum sector livery on 28 March 1993 and was scrapped by M. R. J. Phillips during 1997.

37308, formerly D6608, 37308 and 37274, was built by English Electric Vulcan Foundry during 1965. It is pictured in blue livery on 27 August 2001 and is now privately preserved at the Severn Valley Railway.

37379, formerly D6926 and 37226, was built at English Electric Vulcan Foundry during 1963 and is pictured in Mainline livery on 2 September 2000. 37379 was named Ipswich WRD Quality Approved and was scrapped by C. F. Booth during 2008.

37402, formerly D6974 and 37274, was built by English Electric Vulcan Foundry during 1965 and is pictured in a revised Trainload Freight livery without sector markings on 7 August 2004. 37402 was named *Bont Y Bermo* and is now owned by Direct Rail Services.

37403, formerly D6607 and 37307, was built by English Electric Vulcan Foundry during 1965 and is pictured in a non-standard green livery on 14 March 2000 with 37414. 37403 was named *Ben Cruachan* and is privately preserved at the Bo'ness and Kinneil Railway.

37404, formerly D6986 and 37286, was built by English Electric Vulcan Foundry during 1965 and is pictured in Transrail livery on 25 May 1999. 37404 was named *Loch Long* and was the only Class 37/4 that never worked the Cardiff to Rhymney line after being declared a failure upon arrival at Canton Depot from Weymouth. It was subsequently withdrawn and scrapped by C. F. Booth during 2002.

A set of connecting rods, caps and bolting which have been removed from the power unit of 37406 *The Saltire Society*, undergoing an F exam at Canton Depot on 31 January 2003.

37406, formerly D6995 and 37295, was built by English Electric Vulcan Foundry during 1965 and is pictured in Transrail livery undergoing its F exam on 31 January 2003 with 37417 in the adjacent bay. 37406 was named *The Saltire Society* and was scrapped by C. F. Booth during 2013.

37406, formerly D6995 and 37295, built by English Electric Vulcan Foundry during 1965, is pictured in Transrail livery undergoing its F exam on 31 January 2003. 37406 was named *The Saltire Society* and was scrapped by C. F. Booth during 2013.

37407, formerly D6605 and 37305, was built by English Electric Vulcan Foundry during 1965 and is pictured in Mainline livery on 1 May 1994. 37407 was named *Loch Long* and is now owned by Direct Rail Services.

37408, formerly D6989 and 37289, was built by English Electric Vulcan Foundry during 1965 and is pictured in large logo blue livery on 11 July 1993. 37408 was named *Loch Rannoch* and was scrapped by European Metal Recycling during 2008.

37408, formerly D6989 and 37289, was built by English Electric Vulcan Foundry during 1965 and is pictured in EWS livery on 11 May 2002. 37408 was named *Loch Rannoch* and was scrapped by European Metal Recycling during 2008.

37410, formerly D6973 and 37273, was built by English Electric Vulcan Foundry during 1965. It is pictured in EWS livery on 5 July 2003 and was scrapped by C. F. Booth during 2013.

37412, formerly D6601 and 37301, was built by English Electric Vulcan Foundry during 1965 and is pictured in Transrail livery on 4 October 2002. 37412 was named *Driver John Elliott* and was scrapped by European Metal Recycling during 2012.

37412, formerly D6601 and 37301, was built by English Electric Vulcan Foundry during 1965 and is pictured in Transrail livery on 7 August 2004. 37412 was named *Driver John Elliott* and was scrapped by European Metal Recycling during 2012.

37414, formerly D6987 and 37287, was built by English Electric Vulcan Foundry during 1965 and is pictured in Regional Railways livery on 14 March 2000. 37414 was named *Cathays C. & W. Works 1846–1993* and was scrapped by T. J. Thomson during 2009.

37417, formerly D6969 and 37269, was built by English Electric Vulcan Foundry during 1965. It is pictured in EWS livery undergoing its F exam on 31 January 2003 and was scrapped by C. F. Booth during 2013.

37417, formerly D6969 and 37269, was built by English Electric Vulcan Foundry during 1965. It is pictured in ex-works EWS livery on 5 July 2003 and was scrapped by C. F. Booth during 2013.

37419, formerly D6991 and 37291, was built by English Electric Vulcan Foundry during 1965. It is pictured in EWS livery on 5 July 2003 and is now owned by Direct Rail Services.

37422 *Cardiff Canton*.

37422, formerly D6966 and 37266, was built by English Electric Vulcan Foundry during 1965 and is pictured in ex-works EWS livery following its F exam overhaul and naming ceremony on 31 January 2003. 37422 was named *Cardiff Canton* and is now owned by Direct Rail Services.

37425, formerly D6992 and 37292, was built by English Electric Vulcan Foundry during 1965. It is pictured in Regional Railways livery whilst being temporarily stored at Allied Steel & Wire, Tremorfa Works, on 30 April 2002 and is now owned by Direct Rail Services.

37425, formerly D6992 and 37292, was built by English Electric Vulcan Foundry during 1965 and is pictured in Regional Railways livery on 3 August 2000. 37425 was named *Sir Robert McAlpine / Concrete Bob* and is now owned by Direct Rail Services.

37427, formerly D6988 and 37288, was built by English Electric Vulcan Foundry during 1965. It is pictured in EWS livery on 20 April 2002 and was scrapped by C. F. Booth during 2013.

37428, formerly D6981 and 37281, was built by English Electric Vulcan Foundry during 1965 and is pictured in large logo blue livery on 3 April 1988. 37428 was named *David Lloyd George* and was scrapped by C. F. Booth during 2013.

37428, formerly D6981 and 37281, was built by English Electric Vulcan Foundry during 1965. It is pictured in the Royal Scotsman livery on 31 July 2000 and was scrapped by C. F. Booth during 2013.

37503, formerly D6717 and 37017, was built by English Electric Vulcan Foundry during 1961. It is pictured in EW&S livery on 4 May 2001 and is now privately owned at the Wensleydale Railway.

37503, formerly D6717 and 37017, was built by English Electric Vulcan Foundry during 1961. It is pictured in EW&S livery on 17 August 2001 and is now privately owned at the Wensleydale Railway.

37504, formerly D6739 and 37039, was built by English Electric Vulcan Foundry during 1961. It is pictured in Railfreight grey livery on 29 March 1986 and is now owned by Harry Needle Railroad Company.

37509, formerly D6793 and 37093, was built by English Electric Vulcan Foundry during 1963. It is pictured in Trainload Freight livery with no sector markings on 4 June 2005 and was scrapped by M R. J. Phillips at Canton Depot during 2005.

37512, formerly D6722, 37022 and 37608, was built by English Electric Vulcan Foundry during 1961 and is pictured in Trainload Freight Metals sector livery on 12 April 1994. 37512 was named *Thornaby Demon* and is now owned by the Rail Operations Group.

37517, formerly D6718 and 37018, was built by English Electric Vulcan Foundry during 1961. It is pictured in Loadhaul livery on 30 December 2003 and is now owned by West Coast Railways.

37521, formerly D6817 and 37117, was built by English Electric Vulcan Foundry during 1962. It is pictured in Trainload Freight Petroleum sector livery on 1 May 1994 and is now owned by Locomotive Services Limited.

37675, formerly D6864 and 37164, was built by Robert Stephenson & Hawthorns during 1963 and is pictured in Transrail livery on 19 November 2002. 37675 was unofficially named 'Margam Depot' and was scrapped by European Metal Recycling during 2010.

37677, formerly D6861 and 37161, was built by Robert Stephenson & Hawthorns during 1963. It is pictured in Trainload Freight livery with no sector markings on 28 November 2002 and was scrapped by C. F. Booth during 2008.

37689, formerly D6895 and 37195, was built by Robert Stephenson & Hawthorns during 1963. It is pictured in Trainload Freight livery with no sector markings on 2 September 2000 and was scrapped by European Metal Recycling during 2011.

37694, formerly D6892 and 37192, was built by Robert Stephenson & Hawthorns during 1963. It is pictured in EWS livery at Canton Depot on 3 August 2000 and was scrapped by European Metal Recycling during 2008.

37703 and 37378 are pictured approaching the footbridge at Canton Depot with a Coedbach Washery to Immingham coal train on 9 October 2003. 37703, formerly D6767 and 37067, was built by English Electric Vulcan Foundry during 1962 and is pictured in Trainload Freight Coal sector livery, and is now owned by Harry Needle Railroad Company. 37378, formerly D6904 and 37204, was built by English Electric Vulcan Foundry during 1963 and is pictured in Railfreight Distribution livery, and was scrapped by C. F. Booth during 2009.

37713, formerly D6752 and 37052, was built by English Electric Vulcan Foundry during 1962. It is pictured in Trainload Freight Metal sector livery on 30 December 1988 and was scrapped by Harry Needle Railroad Company during 2007.

37799, formerly D6761, 37061, LO30 and L27, was built by English Electric Vulcan Foundry during 1962 and is pictured in Trainload Freight Coal sector livery on 28 March 1993. 37799 was named *Sir Dyfed / County of Dyfed* and was exported to Spain during 2001 for railway infrastructure work. It was scrapped there in 2011.

37885, formerly D6877, 37177, LO33 and L24, was built by English Electric Vulcan Foundry during 1963 and is pictured in EWS grey undercoat livery on 7 August 1998. 37885 was exported to Spain during 2001 for railway infrastructure work and was scrapped there in 2003.

37887, formerly D6820 and 37120, was built by Robert Stephenson & Hawthorns during 1963. It is pictured in Trainload Freight Petroleum sector livery on 30 December 1988 and was scrapped by C. F. Booth during 2008.

37901, formerly D6850 and 37150, was built by English Electric Vulcan Foundry during 1963 and is pictured in Transrail livery on 2 September 2000. 37901 was named *Mirrlees Pioneer* and is now owned by Europhoenix.

37903 and 37901 are pictured approaching the footbridge at Canton Depot working a Port Talbot to Ebbw Vale steel train on 3 September 1998. 37903 was formerly D6949 and 37149, was built by English Electric Vulcan Foundry during 1964 and is pictured in Trainload Freight Metal sector livery. It was scrapped in Crewe Depot during 2005 (see above for 37901).

37904, formerly D6825 and 37125, was built by Robert Stephenson & Hawthorns during 1963. It is pictured in Trainload Freight Metal sector livery on a low loader in the brickyard sidings opposite Canton Depot on 1 November 2002 and was scrapped at C. F. Booth during 2004.

40122, formerly D200, was built by English Electric Vulcan Foundry during 1958. It is pictured in green livery at the Open Day on 6 July 1985 and is preserved by the National Railway Museum.

47016, formerly D1546, was built by Brush Traction during 1963. It is pictured in Railfreight grey livery on 11 May 1991 and was scrapped by EWS during 2000.

47114, formerly D1702, was built by Brush Traction during 1965. It is pictured in Railfreight Distribution livery on 27 August 1995 and was scrapped by C. F. Booth during 2005.

47194, formerly D1844, was built at Crewe Works during 1965. It is pictured in Railfreight Distribution livery on 22 March 1992 and is now owned by West Coast Railways.

47198, formerly D1848, was built at Crewe Works during 1965. It is pictured in blue livery on 22 March 1992 and was scrapped by Cooper Metals during 1994.

47284, formerly D1986, was built at Crewe Works during 1965. It is pictured in Railfreight Distribution livery on 12 December 1995 and was scrapped by EWS during 1999.

47298, formerly D1100, was built at Crewe Works during 1966 and is pictured in Railfreight Distribution livery on 12 May 1996. 47298 was named *Pegasus* and was scrapped by C. F. Booth during 2007.

47302, formerly D1783, was built by Brush Traction during 1964. It is pictured in Railfreight grey livery with red solebar on 14 June 1997 and was scrapped by T. J. Thomson during 2007.

47365, formerly D1884, was built by Brush Traction during 1965 and is pictured in Railfreight Distribution livery on 11 June 2000. 47365 was named *Diamond Jubilee* and was scrapped by C. F. Booth during 2007.

47480, formerly D1616, was built at Crewe Works during 1964 and is pictured in blue livery on 14 March 1981. 47480 was named *Robin Hood* and was scrapped by Harry Needle Railroad Company during 2001.

47634, formerly D1751 and 47178, was built by Brush Traction during 1964 and is pictured in Rail Express Systems livery without sector markings on 16 March 1998. 47634 was named *Holbeck* and was scrapped by Harry Needle Railroad Company during 2004.

47749, formerly D1660, 47076 and 47625, was built in Crewe Works during 1965 and is pictured in Rail Express Systems livery on 12 April 2002. 47749 was named *Atlantic College* and is now owned by GB Rail Freight.

47776, formerly D1776, 47181 and 47578, was built by Brush Traction during 1964 and is pictured in Rail Express Systems livery on 24 September 2001. 47776 was named *Respected* and is now owned by West Coast Railways.

47901, formerly D1628, 47046 and 47601, was built at Crewe Works during 1964 and is pictured in blue livery on 19 April 1987. 47901 was a test bed for the Class 58 power unit and was scrapped by M. C. Metals during 1992.

50031, formerly D431, was built by English Electric Vulcan Foundry during 1968 and is pictured in large logo blue livery on 14 October 1991. 50031 was named *Hood* and is now privately preserved by the Class 50 Alliance Ltd.

50046, formerly D446, was built by English Electric Vulcan Foundry during 1968 and is pictured in large logo blue livery on 3 April 1988. 50046 was named *Ajax* and was scrapped by M. C. Metals during 1992.

56027 was built by Electroputere during 1977. It is pictured in Loadhaul livery without markings on 26 April 2002 and was scrapped by C. F. Booth during 2009.

56035 is pictured in Loadhaul livery approaching the footbridge at Canton Depot working a Doncaster to Briton Ferry empty coal train on 15 March 1997. 56035 was built at Doncaster Works during 1977 and was scrapped by EWS during 2000.

56035 was built at Doncaster Works during 1977 and is pictured under maintenance on 19 June 1983. 56035 was named *Taff Merthyr* and was scrapped by EWS during 2000.

56038 was built in Doncaster Works during 1977. It is pictured in EWS livery on 24 October 2002 and is now owned by GB Railfreight.

56040 was built in Doncaster Works during 1978 and is pictured in Trainload Freight Metal sector livery on 5 July 1994. 56040 was named *Oystermouth* and was scrapped by T. J. Thomson during 2011.

56047 was built in Doncaster Works during 1978. It is pictured in Civil Engineers livery with Transrail markings on 8 July 1995 and was scrapped by Harry Needle Railroad Company during 2003.

56065 was built in Doncaster Works during 1979. It is pictured in EWS livery on 1 March 2003 and is now owned by GB Railfreight.

56066 was built in Doncaster Works during 1979. It is pictured in Transrail livery on 8 October 1995 and was scrapped by Ron Hull during 2005.

56091 was built in Doncaster Works during 1981 and is pictured in EWS livery on 25 May 2001. 56091 was named *Stanton* and is now owned by DC Rail.

56092 was built in Doncaster Works during 1981. It is pictured in Trainload Freight livery without sector markings on 1 May 1994 and was scrapped by EWS during 2001.

56100 was built in Doncaster Works during 1981. It is pictured in Loadhaul livery on 8 April 2004 and was scrapped by European Metal Recycling during 2010.

56105 is pictured in EWS livery approaching the footbridge at Canton Depot working a Baglan Bay to Immingham tank train on 11 January 2002. 56105 was built in Doncaster Works during 1981 and is now owned by Colas Rail.

56106 was built in Doncaster Works during 1982. It is pictured in Loadhaul livery on 3 December 2002 and is now owned by GB Railfreight.

56109 was built in Doncaster Works during 1982. It is pictured in Loadhaul livery with no markings on 18 September 2002 and was scrapped by T. J. Thomson during 2011.

56113 was built in Doncaster Works during 1982. It is pictured in EWS livery on 1 October 2002 and is now owned by Colas Rail.

56114 was built in Doncaster Works during 1982 and is pictured in Trainload Freight Coal sector livery on 19 June 1993. 56114 is named *Maltby Colliery* and was scrapped by European Metal Recycling during 2012.

56118, pictured in Loadhaul livery, is waiting to leave Canton Isis, opposite Canton Depot, with a freight train to Mossend on 30 April 1999. 56118 was built in Crewe Works during 1983 and was scrapped by C. F. Booth during 2009.

56129 was built in Crewe Works during 1983. It is pictured in Transrail livery on 29 November 2002 and was scrapped by European Metal Recycling during 2011.

57004 was rebuilt from D1828 and 47347 at Brush Traction during 1999. It is pictured in Freightliner livery on 9 September 1999 and is now owned by Locomotive Services Limited.

58003 was built in Doncaster Works during 1983. It is pictured in Railfreight grey livery with red sole bar at the Open Day on 6 July 1985 and was scrapped by European Metal Recycling during 2010.

60001 was built by Brush Traction and entered service during 1991, and is pictured in EWS livery on 23 October 2002. 60001 was named *The Railway Observer* and is owned by DB Cargo.

60011 was built by Brush Traction and entered service during 1991. It is pictured in Mainline livery on 22 November 2002 and is owned by DB Cargo.

60014 was built by Brush Traction and entered service during 1993. It is pictured in Trainload Freight Petroleum sector livery on 25 October 2002. 60014 was named *Alexander Flemming* and is now owned by GB Railfreight.

60015 was built by Brush Traction, entered service during 1993 and is pictured in Transrail livery on 6 May 1995. 60015 is named *Bow Fell* and is owned by DB Cargo.

60026 was built by Brush Traction and entered service during 1990. It is pictured in EW&S livery on 28 November 2002 and is now owned by GB Railfreight.

60033 was built by Brush Traction, entered service during 1991 and is pictured in Corus livery on 13 November 2002. 60033 was named *Tees Steel Express* and is owned by DB Cargo.

60034 was built by Brush Traction and entered service during 1990. It is pictured in Transrail livery on 24 June 2002 and is owned by DB Cargo.

60046 was built by Brush Traction and entered service during 1991. It is pictured in Trainload Freight livery with no sector markings on 3 September 2002. 60046 was named *William Wilberforce* and is now owned by DC Rail.

60051 is pictured in EWS livery approaching Canton Depot bridge with a Margam to Ebbw Vale steel train on 20 May 1998. 60051 was built by Brush Traction, entered service during 1991 and is owned by DB Cargo.

60054 was built by Brush Traction, entered service during 1991 and is pictured in Trainload Petroleum sector livery on 25 October 2002. 60054 was named *Charles Babbage* and is owned by DB Cargo.

60057 was built by Brush traction, entered service during 1991 and is pictured in Trainload Coal sector livery on 2 April 1995. 60057 was named *Adam Smith* and is now owned by DC Rail.

60066 was built by Brush Traction, entered service during 1991 and is pictured in Trainload Freight Coal sector livery with Transrail markings on 11 July 2000. 60066 was named *John Logie Baird* and is owned by DB Cargo.

60068 was built by Brush Traction, entered service during 1991 and is pictured in Trainload Freight livery with no sector markings on 18 May 2002. 60068 was named *Charles Darwin* and is owned by DB Cargo.

60070 is pictured in Trainload Freight livery with Loadhaul sector markings approaching Canton Depot bridge with a Port Talbot to Llanwern iron ore train on 6 July 2000. It was built by Brush Traction and entered service during 1991. 60070 was named *John Loudon McAdam* and is now owned by DC Rail.

60073 was built by Brush Traction and entered service during 1991. It is pictured in Trainload Freight livery with Mainline sector markings on 18 March 2000 and is owned by DB Cargo.

60076 was built by Brush Traction and entered service during 1991. It is pictured in Trainload Freight livery with Mainline sector markings on 20 August 2000 and is now owned by GB Railfreight.

60089 was built by Brush Traction, entered service during 1992 and is pictured in ex-works EWS livery on 7 June 2002. 60089 was named *The Railway Horse* at the Severn Valley Railway on 8 June 2002 and is owned by DB Cargo.

60089 was built by Brush Traction, entered service during 1992 and is pictured in EWS livery on 11 June 2002. 60089 was named *The Railway Horse* and is owned by DB Cargo.

66102 was built by Electro-Motive Diesel during 1999. It is pictured in EWS livery on 12 September 2002 and is owned by DB Cargo.

66172 was built by Electro-Motive Diesel during 1999 and is pictured in EWS livery on 27 August 2001. Its canopy has been removed whilst undergoing alternator repairs.

67002 was built by Alstom Meinfesa during 1999 and is pictured in EWS livery on 12 September 2002. 67002 was named *Special Delivery* and is owned by DB Cargo.

67004 was built by Alstom Meinfesa during 1999 and is pictured in EWS livery on 3 November 2002. 67004 was named *Poste Haste* and is owned by DB Cargo.

67007 was built by Alstom Meinfesa during 1999. It is pictured in EWS livery on 9 June 2000 and is owned by DB Cargo.

67009 was built by Alstom Meinfesa during 1999. It is pictured in EWS livery on 11 June 2000 and is owned by DB Cargo.

67013 was built by Alstom Meinfesa during 2000. It is pictured in EWS livery on 18 February 2001 is and owned by DB Cargo.

67015 was built by Alstom Meinfesa during 2000. It is pictured in EWS livery on 3 October 2002 and is owned by DB Cargo.

67017 was built by Alstom Meinfesa during 2000 and is pictured in EWS livery on 29 April 2002. 67017 was named *Arrow* and is owned by DB Cargo.

67023 was built by Alstom Meinfesa during 2000. It is pictured in EWS livery on 2 September 2000 and is now owned by GB Railfreight.

67023 was built by Alstom Meinfesa during 2000. It is pictured in EWS livery on 11 June 2000 and is now owned by GB Railfreight.

67026 was built by Alstom Meinfesa during 2000. It is pictured in EWS livery on 28 November 2002 and is owned by DB Cargo.

67028 was built by Alstom Meinfesa during 2000. It is pictured in EWS livery on 22 November 2002 and is owned by DB Cargo.

73123 was built by English Electric Vulcan Foundry during 1966 and is pictured in Inter City livery with large logo at the Open Day on 6 July 1985. 73123 was named *Gatwick Express* and is now owned by GB Railfreight and renumbered 73963, following its rebuild at Brush Traction.

One of the painters applying an EWS vinyl to ex-works 08951 on 5 July 2003.

Staff have traditionally placed a nesting bird on the roofs of locomotives to flag up to management that they have spent far too long in the depot awaiting repairs. This picture incensed me to cartoon it on my website along the lines of, 'a Mengel-Dactyl migrating from Jurassic Park has landed on the roof of 67023 and made its nest'. Not everyone was humoured by the cartoon and senior management from Doncaster arranged a visit to the depot only to find that the 'bird' had fled and 67023 had been hastily repaired using parts from 67017 that was also undergoing maintenance.

A view taken from the east end of Canton Depot on 5 July 2003.

A view taken from the west end of Canton Depot on 13 August 2003.

Several Class 37s and a Class 60 inside the Heavy Maintenance Depot on 22 March 1992.

A view looking towards the old coaling tower at the east end of Canton Depot, taken from the footbridge on 24 May 1981.

A view looking towards the old coaling tower at the east end of Canton Depot, taken from the footbridge on 31 May 1979.

D3183 was built was built at Derby Works during 1955. It is pictured in green livery on 29 March 1986 and was scrapped by the National Coal Board during 1987.

Some of the management and staff pose for pictures following the naming ceremony of 37422 *Cardiff Canton* on 31 January 2003.

The senior management of Canton Depot pose for pictures following the naming ceremony of 37422 *Cardiff Canton* on 31 January 2003.

The Shunter Gang pose for pictures with retired fitter Fred Billet following the naming ceremony of 08951 *Fred* on 21 July 2003.

RAILWAYS AROUND THE FENS

JOHN JACKSON

AMBERLEY

First published 2024

Amberley Publishing
The Hill, Stroud
Gloucestershire, GL5 4EP

www.amberley-books.com

ISBN 978 1 3981 1783 9 (print)
ISBN 978 1 3981 1784 6 (ebook)

British Library Cataloguing in Publication Data.
A catalogue record for this book is available from the British Library.

Typesetting by SJmagic DESIGN SERVICES, India.
Printed in the UK.

Contents

Introduction

I can still recall my one and only railway journey to the Cambridgeshire town of Wisbech. It was in the mid-1960s, shortly before the withdrawal of all railway services to the town widely regarded as the capital of the Fens. To a young boy, the flat marshland on this rail journey was regarded as 'boring'. I was soon to realise that, far from this being the case, this area of eastern England, referred to as 'The Fens' or 'Fenland', has a charm all of its own. It accounts for my regular visits to the area spanning well over half a century.

This low-lying Fenland area covers parts of Cambridgeshire, Norfolk and Lincolnshire, with most of the land lying within a few metres of sea level, inland from the Wash. In common with most of the UK, the area lost a number of passenger railway lines just before or as a result of the Beeching Report in the 1960s. The town of Wisbech was one of the more high-profile casualties, losing all passenger services by the end of that decade. The subject of reopening the line between Wisbech and March enjoys a raised profile from time to time, but to date no firm proposals have been submitted.

Likewise, the town of Spalding was once a busy railway junction, with passenger lines extending to all points of the compass from the Lincolnshire town. Today, it is simply a stop on the one surviving line through the town, linking Peterborough and Lincoln via Sleaford.

The direct line linking March to Spalding was to be another line closure in the area, albeit surviving until the early 1980s. There seems to have been an almost deliberate 'plan' to achieve this end, with the passenger-train timings in place ahead of its demise. My trusty notebook of the time recalls a day return trip from March to Spalding one afternoon in autumn 1981. By then, the service had been reduced to just three passenger trains each way on weekdays. Worse, the timings of these made no sense to potential passengers, with no convenient 9 a.m. to 5 p.m. offering for any potential commuters. I caught the last diesel multiple unit of the day, departing March just after 3 p.m. to make the journey of around half an hour to Spalding. I was forced to then return from Spalding on the next, and last, service of the day towards March. That train left just after 6 p.m. The twenty-first-century rail option for any potential travellers between March and Spalding is a circuitous journey via a change of train and passenger operator at Peterborough.

The line linking March with the towns of Chatteris and St Ives was another one to fall victim to closure following the Beeching Report, with passenger services ceasing in 1967.

Further north, the former railway line almost due east of Spalding to the Norfolk town of King's Lynn was an integral part of the Midland & Great Northern Joint

Railway. It was to be one of the casualties ahead of the Beeching era. Spring 1959 saw the closure of this line, depriving places such as Holbeach and Sutton Bridge of all passenger services, with freight facilities being withdrawn a few years later.

In this publication we take a look at those lines that have survived, providing a blend of freight and passenger services in twenty-first-century Fenland. With the Wash as a natural boundary, these lines are framed by Skegness, King's Lynn and Ely to the east with Lincoln, Peterborough and Cambridge to the west.

Passenger services in this area are operated by four companies in this privatised railway era. Greater Anglia operate the majority of services within East Anglia, including stopping services on the Fen Line between Peterborough, Ely and Cambridge. East Midlands Railway are responsible for long-distance services linking Liverpool, Nottingham and Norwich that cross the area covered in this book. Additionally, the same company serve the area linking Lincoln, Sleaford, Boston and Skegness. The 'Great Northern' branded trains are provided by Govia Thameslink Railway, operating services linking King's Lynn, Ely, Cambridge and London King's Cross. The quartet is completed by Arriva's CrossCountry Trains with services linking Birmingham New Street and Stansted Airport.

As a footnote, the Peterborough area was highlighted in some detail in my earlier publication from Amberley Publishing, *Trains Around Peterborough*. Passenger services operated entirely on the East Coast Main Line have therefore been excluded here. Likewise, the wider East Anglia area was covered in my Amberley title *East Anglian Traction*.

The freight traffic in the area is, not surprisingly, dominated by container trains to and from Felixstowe. Much of this traffic from the Suffolk port is routed across East Anglia in order to reach Peterborough and beyond. Volumes are routinely described in 'Twenty-foot Equivalent Units' (TEUs), or 20-foot-long shipping containers, which can easily be transferred by different modes of transport. The Port of Felixstowe currently moves around 1 million TEUs by rail annually. This is the equivalent of saving 100 million HGV miles per year.

These services are operated by three of the country's major freight companies, namely DB Cargo, Freightliner and GB Railfreight. Together they account for around 30 per cent of all domestic container movements by rail, with more than seventy services in and out of the port each weekday. In addition, the Fens' railways see a number of aggregate trains pass through the area on workings originating from the quarries of Leicestershire and Derbyshire. These include regular appearances of DC Rail's small fleet of freight locomotives. Other examples of freight traffic in the area include the regular workings to and from the sand-loading facility at Middleton Towers. Now owned by Sibelco, these freight trains operate on a short spur of the former King's Lynn to Swaffham passenger line.

The town of March has long been a prime railway location in the heart of the Fens, with longstanding historical connection with the evolution of the railways. At one time, the station was served by a total of seven platforms, including bays. Today, it stands with just two platforms in use as a shadow of its former self. Despite its rural location, it is its former importance as a freight centre that secures its place in railway

history. The railway yard at Whitemoor occupied around 250 acres in the town and was, at one time, the largest marshalling yard in the UK. Inevitably the changing methods of handling freight on our railways led to the yard's demise and eventual closure. That was in the 1990s and, since then, changing methods of a different kind have seen the yard reopened in 2004, albeit on a much smaller scale. Today, it serves as the country's leading materials recycling centre. Most of these materials are brought in or despatched by rail, bringing trains to the Fens from a variety of locations around the country.

As I've already said, I have excluded the majority of traffic using the East Coast Main Line. That said, the Fenland railways of rural Lincolnshire have benefited from this main line operating close to its passenger capacity. This has led to an increasing number of freight trains using the alternative route between Peterborough and South Yorkshire via Lincoln on a daily basis. Whilst Sleaford freight traffic bypasses the passenger station via the station's avoiding line, the town of Spalding sees a regular flow of freight trains though its platforms.

On another positive note for the railways of Lincolnshire, Boston docks has recently seen a resurgence of railborne traffic. A DB Cargo-operated service links the docks with the Midlands steel terminal at Wolverhampton, with traffic operated either direct between the two, or via the depot's yards at Toton.

Our journey around the Fens commences at King's Lynn and follows a broadly clockwise direction ending in the Lincolnshire seaside terminus of Skegness. Inevitably, our review of the region majors on a detailed look at the 'core' route between Peterborough and Ely via March.

As always, I hope you enjoy your journey through these pages as much as I have enjoyed compiling them.

Map of the Fens Area Covered in this Book

The Fens, including the areas of Norfolk, Cambridgeshire and Lincolnshire covered in this publication. Our journey starts in King's Lynn and follows a broadly clockwise direction round to Skegness.

Setting the Scene

Our journey around the Fens' railways is, broadly, a clockwise one starting in the town of King's Lynn. The Norfolk town is around 100 miles from London and was once served by locomotive-hauled express trains to the capital, often Class 37-loco-hauled, with a number even offering restaurant car facilities. The town saw electrification in the early 1990s, with an electric unit service to the UK capital surviving to this day.

My fascination with the area's railways is summed up in this scene taken in 2022. The busy line between Peterborough, March and Ely is at the very core of the area's railways. Against the backdrop of a variety of modern traction passing through, the area remains in a sort of 'timewarp', as seen here at Manea. Signal boxes, manually operated level crossings and semaphore signals have survived into the 2020s. Only the Class 755 unit dates this view to the twenty-first century!

A closer search of the area's railway infrastructure can also reveal further examples of days gone by. This London North Eastern Railway sign, for example, remains in situ at March East Junction.

The open view across the flat fenland is clearly demonstrated in this January 2020 view. Both trees and intrusive fences are notorious by their absence. In a typical scene near Manea, East Midlands Trains Class 156 diesel unit No. 156416 is seen on a Nottingham to Norwich service.

A few months later, a local passenger train, operated by Greater Anglia, passes close to the same location. Their unit, No. 755338, crosses the Fens on a Peterborough to Ipswich stopping service.

Our clockwise journey will conclude at the popular Lincolnshire coastal town of Skegness. In its heyday, it was busy conveying passengers to the seaside, a trend that slowed considerably as holidaying habits changed in the second half of the twentieth century. Today, it retains a rail service in the form of hourly trains to and from Nottingham.

King's Lynn to Littleport

In common with the rest of the UK generally, the town of King's Lynn saw considerable rail cutbacks during the 1950s and 1960s. The town's station at South Lynn was closed, together with the lines to Hunstanton and Wisbech. The service to Dereham was also withdrawn with just a short section of track retained to Middleton for freight use. Today, the sole survivor is the Great Northern service to Ely, Cambridge and London. On 15 June 2023, Nos 387115 and 387111 wait to form a service to London King's Cross.

On 12 October 2016, King's Lynn station was used to stable the empty coaching stock of a private charter from London Victoria to Watlington, 6 miles to the south. The leading loco, No. 67012, is seen at the buffer stops.

At the 'London' end of the Pullman coaching stock was No. 67006 *Royal Sovereign*. The train was to leave shortly in order to pick up its return passengers at Watlington.

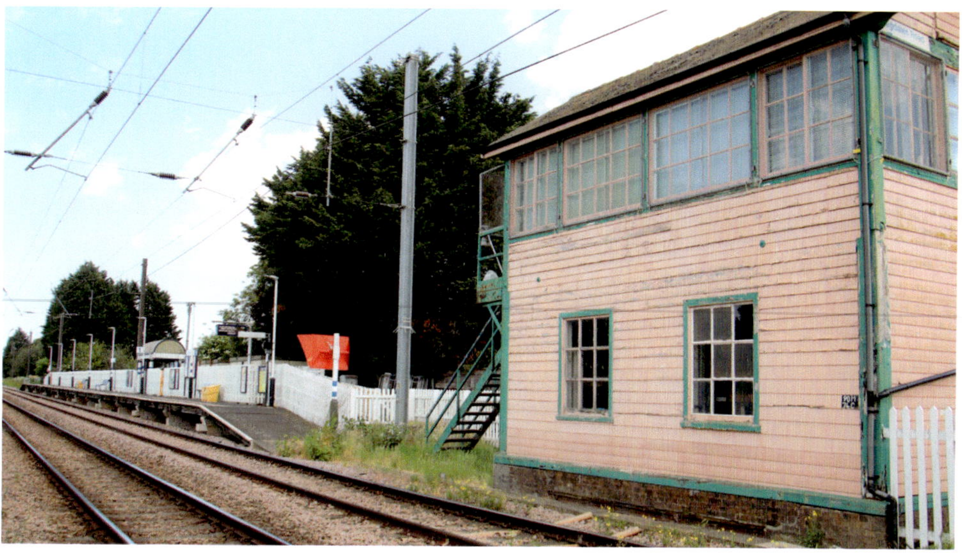

Three Fen Line stations survive between King's Lynn and Ely, the first being at Watlington, 6 miles from King's Lynn. Originally closed along with the Wisbech line in the late 1960s, the station was reopened in 1975 under its previous name of Magdalen Road. It was to be renamed Watlington around 1990, although the signal box retains the original Magdalen Road name and 'Network South East' colours. The platforms are staggered and this is the view of the southbound one in June 2023.

The station at Downham Market, 5 miles further south. On 15 June 2023, a pair of Class 387 units, Nos 387172 and 387121, call on a London King's Cross service.

A little further south, another pair of Class 387 units, Nos 387305 and 387304, pass Ten Mile Bank on the same day. This location is close to the former station at Hilgay, which closed at the end of the 1960s.

The third station from King's Lynn is at Littleport, about 20 miles from King's Lynn. On 2 May 2015, No. 365505 approaches the station on a King's Cross service.

Looking in the opposite direction, the evidence of a bygone era remains even in this 2023 view. The signal box is still in use and the level crossing gates are manually operated by the signalman.

Regular freight traffic in the King's Lynn area is confined to sand trains being operated to and from Middleton Towers, on the former branch line from King's Lynn to Dereham. On 12 October 2016, GB Railfreight's Class 66 locomotive, No. 66762, waits on the branch-line curve at King's Lynn on a loaded working to Barnby Dun, near Doncaster. This working is a longstanding flow operated on behalf of Sibelco.

A second sand working is operated by Freightliner on behalf of Encirc, and links Middleton Towers with Ince & Elton in Cheshire. On 15 June 2023, No. 66623 heads through Littleport with a working from Middleton Towers.

Around Ely and Cambridge

The rail corridor across East Anglia, and Ely and the Fens in particular, is one of the country's busiest. As will be seen in later pages, single-track sections and semaphore signalling are hampering any increase in an already substantial level of freight movements. Of course, passenger trains must also be handled and sometimes 'twice'. This is the case with East Midlands Trains' unit No. 158813, on a Nottingham to Norwich service on 18 August 2018. Its reversal in Ely's platforms means duplicated use of the tracks close to the station.

In addition to East Midlands Trains (now East Midlands Railway), three other passenger operators serve the city of Ely. These are CrossCountry Trains, Great Northern and Greater Anglia. On 13 May 2021, CrossCountry unit No. 170105 calls at Ely on a Stansted Airport to Birmingham New Street service.

The city of Ely is best known for its magnificent cathedral which dominates the skyline of the Fens for miles around. It is also an important railway junction to all parts of East Anglia. Solving the rail capacity issues around Ely is key to the rail-freight operators having any competitive force against the road-haulage industry, particularly in movements to and from the port of Felixstowe. Against the impressive backdrop of the cathedral, GB Railfreight's No. 66755 *Tony Berkeley OBE RFG Chairman 1997–2018* awaits the 'off' on an intermodal from Masborough to Felixstowe on 20 July 2017.

Great Northern (GN) operate services towards King's Lynn to the north and from Ely to Cambridge and London King's Cross to the south. In 2017, Class 365 units were still used on these services. On 1 September that year, No. 365517 is on the rear of an eight-car train calling at Waterbeach station, 5 miles to the north of Cambridge.

Greater Anglia (GA) operate local services linking Ely and Cambridge with other East Anglian towns and cities, notably Peterborough, Norwich and Ipswich. On 13 May 2021, GA unit No. 755413 is seen arriving at Ely on a service from Peterborough to Ipswich.

After thirty years of privatised railways, there have been many historic operators of passenger services in the Fens area. Space here precludes a detailed account of all franchisees and their rolling stock. On 28 August 2007, 'One'-liveried single-car unit No. 153314 makes a call at Ely.

Another single-car Class 153 unit, No. 153306, is seen tucked on the rear of this three-car working on 12 October 2016. Two-car Class 156 unit No. 156416 leads the train as it arrives at Ely. The vast majority of both diesel and electric multiple units formerly operating in the Greater Anglia area have been replaced in the last few years.

The layout of the three-platformed station at Ely can be seen in this view taken from the nearby level crossing on 18 August 2018. The 'main' line south-westwards towards Cambridge can be seen, whilst just out of picture a single line towards Soham and across to Ipswich and Felixstowe veers south-eastwards (to the left) shortly after the station.

One of the station's proud artefacts is the 'Ely Cathedral' nameplate. The name was applied to one of the areas Brush Type 4 Class 47 diesel locomotives, numbered 47572, amongst others. The Class 47 was scrapped at Wigan in 2000, but the name lives on and is now mounted on one of Ely station's platform walls.

The small fleet of Greater Anglia's Class 170 diesel multiple units have now been displaced. On 20 July 2017, No. 170202 stands in one of Cambridge's north-facing bay platforms about to form a service to Norwich.

Sister unit No. 170208 was chosen to carry a promotional livery for East Anglia's 'The Brecks Line'. This branding refers to the 50-mile line linking Cambridge and Norwich, via Ely. On 12 October 2016, the unit is seen calling at Ely.

In May 2017, a new three-platform Fen Line station was opened close to Cambridge Science Park in the suburb of Chesterton. This view of Cambridge North was taken just a few days after opening, with No. 317513 stabled at the north end of the station's terminating platform.

Down at platform level on the same day, a pair of Class 387 units, with No. 387128 leading, can be seen passing on a Great Northern service bound for London King's Cross.

The Fen Line between Cambridge and Ely sees regular Network Rail Test Trains, bringing Colas Rail's Class 37 diesel locomotives to the area. On 20 August 2020, No. 37254 *Cardiff Canton* leads a Cambridge to Great Yarmouth and return working.

These Network Rail Test Trains often feature pairs of Colas Class 37s working in top 'n' tail mode. On this occasion, sister loco No. 37175 is seen bringing up the rear as the train passes close to Waterbeach station.

On arrival from their Derby base, these trains often stable overnight in the sidings to the north of Cambridge station. On 20 July 2017, No. 37116 is seen stabled at the buffer stops awaiting its next duties.

On that occasion, its partner was British Railways' green-liveried celebrity, D6757. The English Electric loco, built in 1962, gained the number 37057 on its transfer to the TOPS numbering system in the 1970s.

High Speed Trains (HSTs) also take their turn in visiting Cambridge on these Network Rail workings. On 5 October 2015, for example, No. 43013 made an appearance and is seen stabled in the same sidings.

Other than these Colas and Network Rail workings, there are far less loco movements through Cambridge than further north. One working, which was in the hands of DB Cargo at the time, is the regular infrastructure working between Whitemoor Yard, in March, and Hoo Junction, in Kent. On 8 June 2012, No. 66023 passed as a light engine move.

Papworth Sidings, on the outskirts of Ely, has been used for storage of a variety of rolling stock in the last few years. On 12 October 2016, Rail Operations Group's No. 37884 *Cepheus* is seen approaching Ely station with a stock move to Papworth Sidings.

On this occasion, the move involved a Class 442 electric multiple unit formerly with South West Trains. The unit, No. 442424, was being moved from Eastleigh to Ely for further storage.

A few minutes earlier the same day, a one-off Freightliner light engine passed through Ely station. Their Class 66 locomotive, No. 66585, then named *The Drax Flyer,* is running from Washwood Heath, in Birmingham, to Parkeston Quay, Harwich.

When this photo was taken on 9 September 2003, local services in East Anglia were in the hands of Anglia Railways, including a small fleet of ten two-car Class 150 diesel multiple units, carrying their turquoise livery. On that date, No. 150237 calls at Ely on a service to Ipswich.

Two decades later, an eight-car electric multiple unit stands in Ely station. On 13 May 2021, Great Northern-operated No. 700026 waits to return to London.

To the south-east of Ely, the line onwards to Bury St Edmunds, Ipswich and Felixstowe branches off on a single-track section through the village of Barway. DB Cargo's No. 66014 passes on an intermodal from Wakefield to Felixstowe. The date was September 2017.

This Freightliner pairing of No. 66567 and No. 66534 *OOCL Express* was also heading to the Suffolk port of Felixstowe. Their rake of container flats had started out from Lawley Street, in Birmingham.

The timetabling for both eastbound workings had to allow for a GB Railfreight working heading in the opposite direction. Their Class 66 loco, No. 66709 *Sorrento*, was in charge of this service from Felixstowe to the terminal at Hams Hall, in the West Midlands. Just twenty-five minutes separated the passing of these three freight services despite the constraints of a single-track section.

The town of Soham lies 7 miles from Ely. Its passenger station was originally closed over half a century ago, in 1965. At a cost of more than £18 million, a single-platform station was reopened in late 2021. The finishing touches were still being added at the time of this photo on 6 January 2022.

The station is served by local Greater Anglia trains between Ipswich and Peterborough. There are signs of some passengers as No. 755415 calls on an Ipswich-bound service that January afternoon. Sadly, the service frequency is restricted to a train every two hours. Would-be rail users were being tempted by free car parking for the initial reopening period.

The Wakefield Euro Terminal to Felixstowe container train is seen again a little earlier that day. It is just about to leave the single-track section as it passes through Soham station. The train is hauled by DB Cargo's No. 66063.

Leaving the double-track section and heading in the opposite direction is GB Railfreight's No. 66743. It is about to head through Soham station on an intermodal service from Felixstowe to Tinsley, near Sheffield.

To the east of Ely, the first station on the line towards Norwich is at Shippea Hill. With an extremely limited service of one or two trains a day, it is hardly surprising that it has one of the lowest annual passenger volumes in the whole of the UK. On 2 May 2015, No. 170205 passes through on a non-stop service to Cambridge.

The second station out of Ely is at Lakenheath. The limited calling of trains and low usage apply here, too, with a weekend service only. Although there is a sizeable community in Lakenheath, it is several miles away and the station is adjacent to the RSPB nature reserve at Lakenheath Fen. East Midlands Trains' No. 158863 passes through on 2 May 2015.

North-westwards from Ely to Manea

The village of Chettisham lies a little further north from Papworth Sidings (which are on Queen Adelaide Way, Ely) on the line towards March and Peterborough, just after the line's fork to King's Lynn. On 1 September 2017, DB Cargo's No. 66121 passes on an eastbound aggregate working from Mountsorrel Quarry, in Leicestershire.

A few minutes later, No. 170270 passed Chettisham on a service to Peterborough. The original station here closed to passengers permanently in the early 1960s, but the site was again used briefly in 1991/1992 when temporary platforms were used in conjunction with the closure of Ely's station during electrification work.

Three miles from Ely, the station at Little Downham also closed in the 1960s, although its name had been changed to Black Bank as long ago as the mid-nineteenth century. CrossCountry Trains' unit No. 170107 passes closes to the former station site on 17 February 2022.

Greater Anglia's No. 755401 is seen passing the same location near Little Downham. This Fenland area offers open-country scenes with few trees and obtrusive fences to obstruct the view.

The line between Ely, March and Peterborough is one of the busiest freight lines in the country, with the majority of traffic seeing containers transported to and from Felixstowe. These services are operated by three of the biggest freight operators in the UK, including DB Cargo. Their Class 66 loco, No. 66080, is seen passing North Fen, Little Downham, on a service from East Midlands Gateway to Felixstowe.

The container traffic is supplemented with a number of aggregate workings into the East Anglia region, including this Freightliner working hauled by No. 66614, heading for Brandon, in Norfolk. For some reason the train had laid over at Oakham loop prior to heading eastward. The date is also February 2022 and the location is again at Little Downham.

The station at Manea remains open albeit with a Greater Anglia service between Peterborough and Ipswich calling here every two hours in each direction. East Midlands Trains' services pass without stopping. On 30 August 2017, their unit, No. 158812, approaches the platform on a Liverpool to Nottingham and Norwich service.

The facilities at Manea station are limited. That said, a glimpse of the interior of the tiny waiting room on the Ely-bound platform is like an Aladdin's cave as this view demonstrates.

The Peterborough to Ely line retains a number of manually operated crossings, signal boxes and semaphore signals. These include the signal box guarding the crossing adjacent to Manea station. This view was taken in May 2020.

Whilst Class 158 units currently operate the majority of the Norwich to Liverpool services, Class 156 units do make regular appearances. On 10 August 2021, No. 156408 passes Manea on a westbound service from Norwich.

On 10 August 2018, a pair of Class 170 units pass close to Manea station. On the left, CrossCountry Trains' unit No. 170637 is seen heading west on a Stansted Airport to Birmingham New Street service. It has just passed Greater Anglia's No. 170270 heading east on a Peterborough to Ipswich service.

The latest Greater Anglia traction contrasts starkly with the bygone feel of the approach to the village station at Manea. On 9 June 2022, No. 755331 slows to make its call on a service to Peterborough.

By contrast to the modern stock above, GB Railfreight's No. 66733 *Cambridge PSB* was called upon to haul a rake of coaching stock heading to the scrapyard on 26 May 2020. A rake of six coaches was seen being moved from the Mid-Norfolk Railway, at Dereham, to Booth Roe's yard at Rotherham.

As already inferred, this busy line across the Fens sees a continuous flow of container trains. On 30 August 2017, it's the turn of GB Railfreight's No. 66766 to pass through Manea station platforms on a Felixstowe to Masborough working.

The same day sees Freightliner's No. 66420 heading in the opposite direction through Manea station. It is heading for Felixstowe on a working from the company's terminal at Stourton, on the outskirts of Leeds.

Freightliner's former Heavy Haul-dedicated Class 66 locos also make regular appearances across the Fens. On a day of winter sunshine, No. 66606 is returning a rake of hoppers to the quarry at Tunstead in Derbyshire. On 18 January 2023 it passes Manea returning from unloading at Kennett, Cambridgeshire.

An intriguing choice of routing occurred as a one-off on 28 April 2021. Freightliner's No. 66567 passed Manea hauling a rake of side-tipper wagons from Westbury Yard to Parkeston Quay, Harwich.

This section of Fenland railway often sees wagon turning moves for traffic emanating from the nearby yard at Whitemoor in March. On 26 May 2020, No. 66542 leads a rake of long welded rail carriers, which are returning to Whitemoor after the train was turned using the triangle of lines at Ely.

These trains necessitate the use of two locos operating in top 'n' tail mode. On this occasion it is No. 66413 *Lest We Forget* bringing up the rear. This is one of Freightliner's locos now carrying the livery of parent company Genesee & Wyoming.

One of the potential Freightliner movements through the Manea area links Whitemoor and Parkeston Quay at Harwich. It only operates on an 'as required' basis but turned up trumps on 5 October 2021. No less than three locos were involved in the light engine move that day. Freightliner's Nos 66553, 66572 and 66548 are seen heading to Parkeston Quay.

Just one solitary tree obstructs the view of the open countryside as No. 66077 *Benjamin Gimbert G C* crosses the Fens on 30 March 2021. This DB Cargo working is heading west towards Manea on an intermodal from Felixstowe to the rail terminal at East Midlands Gateway.

A dark, threatening sky provides the backdrop in this view of DB Cargo's No. 66005 *Maritime Intermodal One*, in DB Maritime Blue livery, passing Manea on 25 February 2020. The loco is heading for Felixstowe with a working from the Euro Terminal at Wakefield, West Yorkshire.

Another DB Cargo 'celebrity'-liveried loco was in charge of this eastbound intermodal on 2 August 2022. Sporting its 'Climate Hero' green livery, No. 66004 is seen heading to Felixstowe.

The Fens' railways see regular aggregate traffic operated by the sixth, and smallest, of the railfreight operators, DC Rail. The company operates a regular flow between Chaddesden, in Derby, and Brandon, in Norfolk. The loaded working, headed by No. 60055 *Thomas Barnardo*, passes Manea on 15 June 2023.

On 10 August 2021, sister loco No. 60028 heads in the opposite direction, returning the empty wagons to Chaddesden. This loco now carries the livery of the parent company, Cappagh Group.

Until recently, the regular infrastructure working between Hoo Junction, in Kent, and Whitemoor Yard, at March, was operated by Colas Rail, regularly bringing that company's locos to the Fens. On 6 April 2018, their Class 66 loco, No. 70803, was in charge.

By the date this photo was taken on 28 April 2021, this working was in the hands of GB Railfreight. On this occasion, the Whitemoor-bound working was a light engine move using No. 66790. DB Cargo's Nos 66092 and 66082 were 'hitching a lift', making the trio a colourful convoy.

Having spent a lot of time watching trains across the Fens, the increased share of freight business handled by GB Railfreight is clearly evident. On 9 December 2020, No. 66783 *The Flying Dustman* heads east nearing journey's end on a Peak Forest to Ely working.

On 3 September 2020, GB Railfreight's sister loco, No. 66752 *The Hoosier State*, heads in the opposite direction with a rake of empty hopper wagons returning from Harlow Mill to Bardon Hill quarry in Leicestershire.

March and Whitemoor

The town of March owes its growth to the coming of the railways and continuing to be a railway centre for much of the last century. Its importance as a railway junction reduced with the progressive closure of the lines to St Ives, Wisbech and Spalding. Nevertheless, the station approach still leads to an impressive station entrance building.

Once extending to seven platforms, the station today is one of two halves. Two platforms remain operational, in use serving trains to Peterborough and to Ely. The remaining 'half' is seen here, taken in 2017, showing the abandoned platforms, retained but out of use. Closer examination of these platforms and the station area generally will reveal the hard work being carried out by the Friends of March railway station volunteer group since 2009.

This is the view of March's two operational platforms in August 2017, looking towards Ely. Platform 2 serves Ely and beyond, whilst platform 1 caters for trains towards Peterborough. In the distance, a GB Railfreight Class 66 sits in the goods loop.

Just to the east of the station is March East Junction signal box. The imposing structure, situated next to a busy level crossing, was photographed in August 2017.

CrossCountry Trains serve March with their hourly service linking Birmingham New Street, Cambridge and Stansted Airport. On 30 August 2017, No. 170102 calls on a Birmingham to Stansted working.

Later the same day, No. 170110 is seen approaching March station and passing East Junction signal box. It will continue towards Peterborough, Leicester and Birmingham.

A two-car Class 170 unit approaches the station on an 'all stations' calling service from Ipswich to Peterborough. On this occasion, No. 170271 is in use. These westbound services are timed to follow the faster, longer-distance trains on departure from Ely.

This East Midlands Trains (EMT) unit, No. 158777, is about to pass through March station's platform 1 without stopping. The operator does not regularly serve the town by way of its Norwich to Nottingham and Liverpool workings.

Sister EMT unit No. 158847 is seen heading in the opposite direction as it is about to pass over the station's level crossing. It was a damp day in the Fens on 30 August 2017.

One of Greater Anglia's newest units, No. 755411, passes March South Junction and heads for the town's station on a stopping service to Peterborough. These Class 755 units now handle all of the operator's local diesel services.

The longstanding sand workings from Middleton Towers were in the hands of EWS (DB Cargo) back in March 2013. No. 66024 is in charge in this view. Since then, GB Railfreight has taken over the trains' operation and these short-wheelbase wagons have now been withdrawn.

The new order is seen here in June 2023. GB Railfreight's No. 66703 *Doncaster PSB 1981–2002* is about to pass over March station crossing with a rake of the Sibelco replacement wagons on a service from Middleton Towers to Monk Bretton.

Sister loco No. 66712 *Peterborough Power Signalbox* also passes over the station crossing in this view on 30 August 2017. In a scene now consigned to railway history, this photo was taken prior to these older wagons being replaced.

A number of aggregate trains from the quarries of Leicestershire and Derbyshire cross the Fens in order to serve their various East Anglian destinations. On 13 March 2013, for example, No. 66130 heads east through platform 2 at March station.

Ten years later, in June 2023, sister loco and class pioneer No. 66001 is about to pass over the station crossing on this westbound intermodal from Felixstowe to East Midlands Gateway.

With around seventy container trains in and out of Felixstowe every weekday, it is never long before one such working appears in the Fens. In August 2017, No. 66756 *Royal Corps of Signals* heads this GB Railfreight working from the port as it heads for the Maritime Transport terminal at Doncaster iPort.

Around 30 per cent of all onward domestic container movements from Felixstowe are handled by the main rail operators. Freightliner's Class 70 loco No. 70015 is in charge of this working from Felixstowe to Crewe on the same day.

The freight traffic on this busy line across the Fens has to be scheduled around the frequent passenger services. Westbound services are often held in the loop at March for these purposes. On 30 August 2017, for example, GB Railfreight's No. 66742 *ABP Port of Immingham Centenary 1912–2012* enters the loop with its sand train to enable passenger services to pass.

Loco stabling in the station area has become less common in recent years. Back in March 2013, GB Railfreight's No. 66733 *Cambridge PSB* was to be found in March goods yard.

In the previous photo, No. 66733 can be seen stabled next to a snowplough. March was home to at least one of these ploughs for as long as I can remember. This is a close-up view, taken in 2017, of snowplough numbered ADB965211.

Earlier this century, the former goods shed at March was used for loco servicing. The reopening of the nearby yard at Whitemoor saw an increased focus on the March station area for this purpose.

Much has changed at March in the ten years that separate these two views of the area's sidings and Up yard. This 2013 view shows a short rake of long-stored wagons amongst the vegetation for as long as I can remember. They include 'rudd' numbered 972029, which I first recorded at this location back in 2006!

Those relics have since long gone and the Up yard has been used by GB Railfreight since 2019 for stabling and maintenance of its wagons. It had previously used just the Down yard for these purposes. This is the much tidier site in action in June 2023.

This is the view from March South Junction taken on the same day in 2023. The Down yard is home to a number of former 'HTA' coal hoppers. These former DB Cargo wagons are now seeing alternative uses by GB Railfreight.

The importance of March as a railway centre may have waned since marshalling yards and wagon shunting gave way to block trains. Nevertheless, there has been something of a renaissance here in the last few years. That said, the open spaces for which the Fens are well known are never far away. Less than a mile from the March scenes here, DB Cargo's No. 66168 approaches the outskirts of the town with a Mountsorrel to Kennett aggregate working.

As already mentioned, much of March's freight activity is generated by workings to and from the yard at Whitemoor. This traffic includes an almost daily working from Hoo Junction, in Kent, and its return. In 2017, the then Colas-operated working has just arrived from Hoo Junction and is crossing over to use the Up platform through the station.

At the end of that station platform, the train will veer sharply to the right to make use of a triangle of lines giving entry to Whitemoor Yard via a southern spur.

The main line from Peterborough, which closely avoids the Whitemoor Yard entrance, passes over Norwood Road level crossing. A spur from the main line just north of this point enables trains to and from the Peterborough direction to enter the yard. GB Railfreight's No. 66719 *Metroland* is seen on the crossing in June 2023 on a Doncaster to Felixstowe intermodal service.

Whitemoor Yard was once the biggest marshalling yard in the UK and the second biggest in Europe. It was particularly important in maintaining the supply chain during the Second World War. After a long period out of use, it was reopened in 2004 and has been the rail industry's national recycling centre for the last decade. Today it has a dual purpose. From here, materials are despatched to be used in infrastructure projects and also products are returned here for recycling. This includes a ballast washing facility. This is the view of the entrance to Whitemoor today.

Half a century ago, March housed the biggest traction maintenance depot in East Anglia. Situated close to the Whitemoor marshalling yard and coded '31B' under British Railways, it became 'MR' in 1973 under the British Rail TOPS scheme. On a blisteringly hot August afternoon in 1975, at the height of the days when almost all traction was blue, my first glimpse of the depot area revealed, from left to right, the noses of Nos 31323, 31119 and 25042.

The immediate area around the depot was home to a Class 08 diesel shunter and a number of Class 37 locos, including No. 37064. The level of shunting duties in the mid-1970s was borne out by the presence of no less than ten Class 08s on the depot that afternoon. Sadly, the demise of the Speedlink traffic led to the inevitable closure of the depot in 1992.

Whittlesea and Three Horseshoes

To the west of March lies the tiny village of Turves, which is in an area known for its multiple level crossings within a short distance. The most notable of these is close to Three Horseshoes signal box, seen here in 2017. The location was once a junction, with a short, 4-mile-long branch line to Benwick leaving the main Peterborough to March and Ely line at this point. The branch line closed in 1964.

With the signal box to the left, No. 170271 passes over Three Horseshoes level crossing on 12 December 2017. It is forming a Peterborough to Ipswich service.

East Midlands Trains' No. 158777 is seen in the same view in April 2018. The white building partially concealed by the driving cab is the Three Horseshoes pub on March Road. As this building dates from the mid-nineteenth century it is likely that it has given its name to this extremely rural railway location.

The busy line through this part of the Fens has no surviving loops between Peterborough and to the east of March, unless the working is destined to go into Whitemoor Yard itself, so timetabling is a major factor. DB Cargo's No. 66092 passes Three Horseshoes on 12 December 2017 on a Mountsorrel to Kennett working.

Five minutes later, Freightliner's No. 66594 *NYK Spirit of Kyoto* passes in the opposite direction. Although a short train, this particular working demonstrates the type of 'advertisement' for rail use that, in the author's opinion, should be copied to this day by all train operators. All too often diesel fuel for rail companies' own use is moved to their depots by road transport. Here, empty fuel tanks from Freightliner's use at their Ipswich fuel point are returned to Lindsey, on South Humberside.

Later that afternoon, No. 66523 heads past the signal box over the crossing as it heads east with a Freightliner from Lawley Street, in Birmingham, to Felixstowe. The Three Horseshoes pub can again be seen in the background.

On 6 April 2018, DB Cargo's No. 66171 passes the level crossing on an aggregate service bound for unloading at Papworth Sidings at Ely. The train had originated at Peak Forest, in Derbyshire.

Trains heading west from Whitemoor also contribute to the mix on this section of line across the Fens. The quarry at Mountsorrel, in Leicestershire, is a regular destination of GB Railfreight workings from Whitemoor. On the same day in April 2018, No. 66748 *West Burton 50* has just left the yard on its westbound journey and is approaching the level crossing.

There is something distinctive about the sound of a Class 70 loco breaking the silence of the Three Horseshoes countryside. Sadly, Freightliner's use of Class 70 locomotives on its container trains from Felixstowe has all but ceased. Perhaps scenes like this one of No. 70017 on a service from Felixstowe to Crewe are now a thing of the past. Certainly, this particular morning working across East Anglia and reaching the West Coast Main Line at Nuneaton has ceased to run since early 2023.

The line reaches the small market town of Whittlesey 3 miles to the west of Three Horseshoes. Despite its rural location on a minor road on the edge of town, the level crossing is busy for both road and rail traffic, with the westbound station platform towards Peterborough shown on the left of this view.

The station name has always taken the alternative spelling of 'Whittlesea'. Today, its signage has 'The Hereward Community Rail Partnership' branding. Indeed, the station posters highlight the increasing numbers of passengers, Covid-19 apart, since the partnership was created. Further, the Hereward Line poster encourages readers to 'Take the train from one cathedral city to another – or explore The Fens via Manea, March and Whittlesea. What better way to go!' The line's name derives from the Anglo-Saxon hero Hereward the Wake, who led local resistance to William the Conqueror in the area from the Isle of Ely to the environs of Peterborough.

There can surely be no better place in England to observe the railways' blend of modern trains and past customs. In this January 2019 view the manually operated crossing gates are being handled by the gatekeeper, complete with his own 'hut', which can be seen below the British Rail arrow. The crossing's protective semaphore signal is also visible on the platform end.

The gatekeeper is also within sight of, and no doubt in two-way communication with, the local Whittlesea signalman, whose box is just a few yards away. In August 2022, it looked as if a fresh coat of green paint had been applied to his box.

On 3 August 2020, GB Railfreight's No. 66739 *Bluebell Railway* approaches another of Whittlesea's level crossings, on Ramsey Road, on one of the regular sand trains from Middleton Towers to Monk Bretton, in South Yorkshire.

The two platforms at Whittlesea station are staggered. This is the view from the March-bound platform looking across to No. 66734 Pla*tinum Jubilee* as it heads west through the Peterborough-bound platform on a working from Whitemoor to Mountsorrel.

On 10 August 2021, a Tuesday, Freightliner's revised-liveried No. 66418 *Patriot In Memory Of Fallen Railway Employees* approaches the station on the weekly move of empty fuel tanks between their Ipswich stabling point and Lindsey, South Humberside. This working is usually allocated for a Tuesday each week.

A wagon trip of a different kind is seen here on 5 October 2020. GB Railfreight's No. 66776 *Joanne* is tripping a short rake of their container flat wagons between the company's major hub at Peterborough and the yard at March.

On 30 August 2017, Freightliner's No. 66598 is seen taking the curve as it passes through Whittlesea's open landscape on a container train from Birmingham's Lawley Street terminal to the port of Felixstowe.

By contrast, the dead-straight section of track looking from Whittlesea towards March is evident in this view on 30 March 2020. A Freightliner working from Felixstowe to Crewe, hauled by No. 66508, is seen passing the signal box on its approach to the station.

The summer's vegetation growth partially obscures this working on 30 August 2017. DB Cargo's No. 66118 is in charge of a loaded aggregate service from Mountsorrel quarry, in Leicestershire. The working is heading for unloading at Barham, a few miles from Ipswich, Suffolk.

On 25 February 2020, DB Cargo classmate No. 66125 passes through Whittlesea station as it heads east on another loaded stone working from Mountsorrel.

Another regular GB Railfreight working from Whitemoor Yard is seen on 28 April 2021. Their loco, No. 66711 *Sence*, sporting its Aggregate Industries livery, passes through Whittlesea with a mixed rake of infrastructure wagons destined for Doncaster.

Another pair of GB Railfreight Class 66 locos was involved in this light engine move on 6 August 2020. The company regularly moves its locos between Peterborough and March and on this occasion No. 66754 *Northampton Saints* and No. 66771 *Amanda* passed through the station heading for March.

On 10 October 2021, No. 66712 *Peterborough Power Signalbox* heads through the station on a return working to Felixstowe. This time the train has originated from Tinsley, near Sheffield.

On 16 June 2020, the empty Sibelco sand wagons from Goole to Middleton Towers were booked to operate via a layover in March Yard. GB Railfreight's 'Cemex'-liveried No. 66780 *The Cemex Express* was in charge as it passes the eastbound platform at Whittlesea.

On 10 August 2021, a pair of Class 365 electric multiple units were moved from the storage facilities at Papworth Sidings in Ely to Doncaster. The units involved were Nos 365528 and 365512 (nearer the camera).

This pair of electric units is seen passing Whittlesea signal box being dragged by No. 57310 *Pride of Cumbria*. The unit move was operated by Rail Operations Group.

King's Dyke signal box controls another busy level crossing on the western fringe of Whittlesea. The road traffic on this Peterborough to Whittlesey road suffers long tailbacks when the barriers are down. I have vague recollections of a couple of houses adjacent to this box, but these must have been demolished.

On 1 January 2019, East Midlands Trains' Class 158 unit, No. 158852, speeds past the signal box and over the level crossing on a service from Liverpool and Nottingham to Norwich.

Peterborough

The city lies at the western end of the Hereward Line across the Fens. A detailed account of the diversity of rail traffic in the area around the city can be found in my earlier Amberley publication, *Trains Around Peterborough*. One occasional move that involved crossing the Fens warrants inclusion here. Direct Rail Services' Class 37 No. 37604 is seen approaching Peterborough returning a Greater Anglia Class 90 electric loco, No. 90002, to Norwich Crown Point depot.

Services reaching Peterborough to and from the Fens use the main station today, once called 'North'. This involves snaking round the sharp curves via the site of the former 'East' station. On 1 September 2017, No. 66764 *Major John Poyntz Engineer & Railwayman* is seen rounding these curves on a GB Railfreight intermodal from Felixstowe to Birch Coppice.

A couple of miles north of Peterborough station lies the recently modified junction at Werrington and Marholm. The majority of freight trains from the Fens heading north from here are now routed via the Lincoln line rather than the East Coast Main Line. On 25 February 2022, DB Cargo's No. 66170 approaches this junction heading towards Peterborough and the Fens on a Wakefield Euro Terminal to Felixstowe intermodal. Extensive track rationalisation work was completed at this junction in late 2021. This work should enable freight traffic to join the Spalding line without impeding the movements of faster passenger services on the East Coast Main Line.

Specialist passenger operator West Coast Railway Company operate a number of charter trains from both Ely and Norwich. These passenger workings and the associated empty stock moves often make use of the Fen Line. On 30 November 2014, No. 47760 brings up the rear of a returning empty stock move to Carnforth, which has just crossed the Fens from Ely with No. 57313 leading the train. It is seen here passing Marholm, just north of Peterborough.

Spalding and Sleaford

Our journey around the Fens now takes us over the county boundary into Lincolnshire, and a look at two of the surviving stations in the county, Spalding and Sleaford. The impressive station entrance buildings at Spalding are shown in this April 2018 view. Behind, a different story is told. At one time, the station boasted seven platforms, but today it has just two. This decline started with the closure of the direct line to March in 1982.

Since privatisation, the town's surviving service links Spalding with Peterborough to the south and Sleaford and Lincoln to the north, with East Midlands Railway as the current passenger-service operator. On 11 May 2018, their single-car unit No. 153376 is seen leaving the station.

More recently, Class 170 units are making an increasing number of appearances on these services, particularly with the withdrawal of the Class 153 fleet. On 24 October 2022, No. 170273 approaches Spalding station on a service from Lincoln to Peterborough.

LNER Azumas now operate the majority of long-distance services using the East Coast Main Line (ECML), with this Spalding line used only for planned diversions or other service disruption. On this warm October day in 2022, their unit, No. 800207, passes through Spalding station on a Peterborough to Doncaster run to maintain driver route knowledge of this line.

In order to allow as many high-speed paths as possible on the ECML between Peterborough and Doncaster, most of the freight traffic now uses this route through Spalding. On 11 May 2018, for example, DB Cargo's No. 66059 heads north returning a rake of empty wagons from Bow, East London, and Biggleswade to Heck, in North Yorkshire.

This longstanding freight flow is operated on behalf of Plasmor, a concrete-block and paving manufacturer. The returning empty wagons are seen again on 11 October 2022, this time with No. 66110 in charge.

In May 2018, GB Railfreight's No. 66749, since named *Christopher Hopcroft MBE 60 Years Railway Service*, is in charge of the Middleton Towers to Goole sand train as it powers through Spalding. Goole Glassworks is then reached via Lincoln and a layover at Doncaster.

I don't usually select wall-art photos but a couple of local street artists in Spalding were commissioned to 'brighten up' local commuting from the station. The impressive *Hogwarts Express* now adorns the previously plain wall on Spalding station platform.

The town of Sleaford is approximately 18 miles to the north of Spalding. Unlike its counterpart, Sleaford has a station avoiding line used by freight trains, leaving the station itself to handle passenger workings operated by East Midlands Railway. Their hourly Grantham to Skegness service also calls here, retaining its status as a Lincolnshire crossroads. Three platforms remain in use as a result. This is the view of the station's platforms in March 2020.

The eastern end of Sleaford station is protected by Sleaford East signal box, seen here on the same day in March 2020. I believe Sleaford remains one of the few places with four signal boxes named north, south, east and west still in existence.

Some East Midlands' services remained in the hands of Class 153 single-car diesel units at that time. A pair of these units, Nos 153382 and 153372, is passing the signal box and about to make their Sleaford call.

Inevitably the variety the railway observer has on offer at Sleaford is limited to a selection of just a few diesel unit classes. By way of 'variety', two-car No. 156918, sporting EMR's revised Regional livery, calls that same day.

Shortly after that, it is the turn of a Class 158 two-car unit, No. 158799, to arrive at Sleaford. It is heading for the least-used platform here, platform 3.

Lincoln, Boston and Skegness

The city of Lincoln lies around 20 miles from Sleaford and is in the far north-west corner of the Fens. As mentioned in the previous section, most freight traffic between the railway junctions at Peterborough and Doncaster is now routed through the city's station. On 28 March 2018, Freightliner's No. 66563 passes through on a Leeds to Felixstowe container working.

The same Freightliner container working is double-headed by Nos 66539 and 66572 on 10 March 2020. These services are often used as a means of moving locos between Freightliner's key maintenance and servicing hubs at Leeds and Ipswich.

Lincoln's station, formerly known as Central, lies at the very heart of the city, and is now the only city station since the closure of St Mark's in 1985. Much effort has been made to reduce train movements, particularly unit shunting between platforms, across the busy High Street level crossing. The empty stock from a passenger charter is seen crossing, with No. 66078 on one end of the coaching stock.

We resume our journey through Lincolnshire by moving south-eastwards to pick up the line from Sleaford towards Skegness. The village station at Hubbert's Bridge, 3 miles to the west of Boston, is one of several on the line with an extremely limited stopping service. On 8 August 2023, EMR's No. 170201 passes non-stop on a service towards Boston and Skegness.

The town of Boston is now served by a two-platform station with trains between Nottingham and Skegness. The centre through lines have long been removed as can be seen in this rather forlorn scene at the station area as No. 156413 calls in May 2012.

A decade later and the service 'improvements' include the use of a three-car Class 170 diesel unit on these Poacher Line services. On 8 August 2023, No. 170418, a recent transfer to EMR from ScotRail, calls on a Skegness to Nottingham service. The station has a passing loop with single-track sections to both east and west of here, the result of efforts to reduce track maintenance costs in the 1980s.

The Port of Boston has seen regular rail use in recent years via the steel terminal within Boston Docks, located on the Wash. On 8 August 2020, DB Cargo's No. 60062 *Sonia* approaches West Street Junction signal box with a working from Toton Yard.

The loco will shortly pull forward towards the station platform before reversing towards the docks' swing bridge to enable the trainload to enter the docks complex. It is seen here about to commence its reversal. It will leave the docks later with the loaded train and head to the Victoria Group's steel terminal in the West Midlands.

The BRA and BYA types of steel wagons used on this service were built in the late 1990s and are a welcome alternative to the container flats and aggregate hoppers seen routinely elsewhere in the Fens. BYA, numbered 964023, is seen here in the wagon rake that day.

The line between Grantham and Skegness has been branded as the 'Poacher Line', with promotional poster boards showing the reader what is on offer along the line. This is the example on display at Wainfleet station. The Poacher Line was one of the original pilots under the Department for Transport's Community Rail Schemes.

The market town of Wainfleet All Saints lies 5 miles from the line's terminus at Skegness. Wainfleet station's two platforms, together with its level crossing and signal box, can be seen in this view taken on 7 July 2018.

Later the same day, a pair of East Midlands Trains' Class 156 diesel multiple units, Nos 156497 and 156498, call on a Saturday service from Skegness to Nottingham.

Our journey around the Fens coincides with the end of the Poacher Line at Skegness. With the station's terminus behind the camera, this is the platform end view of the signal box and semaphore signals looking south-west on 11 May 2018.

This view looking towards the buffer stops was taken on the same day. The six platforms remain in situ (technically numbered 2 to 7 as platform 1 was demolished in the 1980s). That said, in practice only platforms 3 and 4 are in regular use. A service formed of No. 158785 is waiting to return to Nottingham.

Loco-hauled trains, once famously involving pairs of Class 20s, are seemingly consigned to history. Charter trains continue to make occasional appearances and, on 5 May 2012, a pair of Class 66s, working in top 'n' tail formation, arrived on the Lincolnshire Coast Express. On that occasion, the loco at the buffer stops was No. 66165, complete with appropriate headboard.